Key to the Problem

Mike Gould

United Kingdom: Folens Publishers, Apex Business Centre, Boscombe Road, Dunstable, LU5 4RL.
Email: folens@folens.com

Ireland: Folens Publishers, Greenhills Road, Tallaght, Dublin 24.
Email: info@folens.ie

Poland: JUKA, ul. Renesansowa 38, Warsaw 01-905.

Editor: Joanne Mitchell

Layout artist: Suzanne Ward

Cover design: John Hawkins

First published 2005 by Folens Limited.

British Library Cataloguing in Publication Data. A catalogue record for this publication is available from the British Library.

ISBN 1 84303 731 9

Contents

The story so far

If you haven't read an *On the edge* book before:
The stories take place in and around a row of shops and buildings called Pier Parade in Brightsea, right next to the sea. There's Big Fry, the fish and chip shop; Drop Zone, the drop-in centre for local teenagers; Macmillan's, the sweet and souvenir shop; Anglers' Haven, the fishing tackle shop; the Surf 'n' Skate shop and, of course, the Brightsea Beach Bar.

If you have read an *On the edge* book you may have met some of these people before.

Sandra King:	*Frankie King's wife; mother to Mick, Sara and Jamie.*
Frankie King:	*Sandra's husband; runs several nightclubs in Brightsea.*
Mick:	*their elder son.*
Sara:	*his sister.*
Jamie:	*his younger brother.*
Mel Slater:	*owner and manager of the 3 Bs. Australian.*

So, what's been going on?
Sandra works at the 3 Bs, helping Mel out, although Frankie disapproves and can't understand why she needs to work. Sandra is getting fed up with Frankie coming and going as he pleases at all hours, even if he says he has to, with his business – running nightclubs.

What happens in this story?
Frankie comes round to the family house one afternoon to give Sandra a gift, but she's out working at the 3 Bs. He leaves it with Sara and asks her to pass on a message to meet him at the Marina. Sandra can't work out why – it's not her birthday, or their anniversary, so what's Frankie up to?

Characters

SANDRA KING

FRANKIE KING: Sandra's husband

MICK KING: their son

SARA KING: their daughter

JAMIE KING: their younger son

MEL SLATER: owner of the 3 Bs

Scene 1

The Kings' living room.

Late afternoon.

SARA on sofa, watching TV. Enter FRANKIE, her father.

SARA: Hi, dad.

FRANKIE: Hi, darling. Where's your mum?

SARA: You just missed her.

FRANKIE: Oh. Where is she?

SARA: She's working at the 3 Bs until 7:00 pm this evening.

FRANKIE: The 3 Bs? She didn't tell me.

SARA: Do you mind, then?

FRANKIE sits down on sofa.

FRANKIE: Nah. No problem. I just wanted to surprise her.

SARA: Surprise her?

FRANKIE: You know – a little gift.

SARA: It's not her birthday, dad.

FRANKIE: I know. Doesn't have to be her birthday, does it?

SARA: No, 'course not. It's nice of you, dad.

She waits.

SARA: So, aren't you gonna tell me?

FRANKIE: Tell you what?

SARA: About the present!

FRANKIE: Sorry, love. It's a secret.

He gets a small envelope out of his pocket.

FRANKIE: Here.

SARA: That's it? The gift?

FRANKIE: Sort of. Look, when she comes in can you give it to her?

SARA: Why can't you?

FRANKIE: I have to be somewhere.

SARA: What shall I tell her?

FRANKIE: Tell her to come to the address. The one on the front of the envelope.

SARA: When?

FRANKIE: Tonight. 8:30 pm.

SARA (*laughs*):
Very mysterious.

FRANKIE: Your mum likes surprises.

SARA: No, she doesn't.

FRANKIE: She'll like this one. (*stands up*) Where are your brothers?

SARA: Jamie's having tea at a friend's. Mum's picking him up later.

FRANKIE: What about Mick?

SARA: How should I know?

FRANKIE: That boy. He needs to leave school and get a decent job.

SARA: What – like you?

FRANKIE: Yeah, that's right. Earning good money.

SARA: I'll tell Mick you were here. If I see him.

She pauses.

SARA: Dad, can I ask you something?

FRANKIE: Go on, love.

SARA: You're never here much now. Even some nights you stay away. Why? Don't you like coming home?

FRANKIE: Don't be silly, love! It's just I have stuff I have to do. Late night meetings. It's easier to sleep in the office sometimes.

SARA: I wish you were here more.

FRANKIE (*looks guilty*):
Look – I gotta go. Maybe this weekend – you and me. We could do something.

SARA: That'd be good.

FRANKIE (*checks watch)*:
See you, love. And don't forget. Give that envelope to your mum when she comes in.

Scene 2

The 3 Bs.

The same time.

MEL behind the bar serving people. SANDRA collecting some 'empties' from the table. The people at the bar go.

MEL: So, how's that husband of yours?

SANDRA: Don't ask! I never see him anymore. Sometimes I think he loves his nightclubs more than me.

MEL: He must be a fool then.

SANDRA: Don't make me blush.

MEL: It's true. Nothing is as important as your family.

SANDRA: So, how come you're on your own?

MEL: I've never met the right woman.

SANDRA walks up to the bar and puts the glasses down.

SANDRA: How could they resist you?

MEL (*laughs*): Easy!

SANDRA (*suddenly sees the time*):
Do you mind? – I have to go at 7:00 pm. Got to pick up Jamie from a friend's.

MEL: No worries. Seems pretty quiet today. I think lots of folk go over to those posh pubs and clubs at the Marina.

SANDRA: Frankie tells me he wants a club there. But I told him, it's not my scene. All those rich types with their boats. I'm happy with a cup of coffee here, looking at the sea.

MEL: Me too.

SANDRA: Frankie does it to impress me. The fast cars, the money, the nightclubs. But it doesn't work. I'd like it if he was at home a bit more.

MEL: He's lucky having three nice kids.

SANDRA: Mick? Nice?

MEL: He'll turn out alright.

SANDRA: I hope so.

A crowd of people come in.

SANDRA: I thought you said it was quiet?

MEL: It was! Until two minutes ago. Can you help me serve?

SANDRA: It's almost 7:00 pm.

MEL: Just give me ten minutes. Can you hang on till Joolz arrives?

SANDRA: I guess so.

MEL: Thanks. I owe you!

Scene 3

The Kings' house.

Early evening.

MICK at the kitchen table. SARA with a frying pan.

MICK: Baked beans in a frying pan?

SARA: Yeah – so what? Tastes the same.

MICK: No, it doesn't.

SARA (*cross*):
You make it then. Don't complain!

MICK: Where's mum?

SARA (*empties beans onto MICK's plate*): Picking up Jamie.

MICK: I need proper food. Not this stuff.

SARA: Fine. Give them here. I'll have them.

MICK: No way! These are mine.

SARA: Oh I see. You like them now.

MICK: They're better than nothing.

MICK takes a huge mouthful of beans and toast.

SARA: You're *gross*!

MICK: Thanks.

SARA: It's *not* funny.

Enter SANDRA with JAMIE.

SANDRA (*to JAMIE*):
Right – straight upstairs and into your pyjamas.

JAMIE (*yawns*):
I'm not tired!

SANDRA: Not much. Go on – off you go.

JAMIE leaves the room.

SARA: Where have you been, mum?

SANDRA: I had to work late. Then I got stuck in traffic. Then Jamie made a scene at his friend's.

MICK: It's gone 8:00 pm, mum. Look what she made me eat!

SANDRA: She?

SARA: He means me.

SANDRA: What do you mean? You've finished it all.

MICK: Only 'cos I would have died of hunger otherwise.

SARA: Huh! Thanks a lot.

SANDRA: Take no notice, love.

SARA: Do you want a cup of tea?

SANDRA: That'd be lovely.

She slumps down into a chair.

SANDRA: Seen your dad?

SARA: Oh – I almost forgot. He was here earlier. About 4:00 pm. He left something for you …

SANDRA: Oh?

SARA: Here.

She hands her mum the envelope.

SANDRA (*reads the front*): '73 Harbour Court, Green Harbour Way'.

She opens the envelope.

MICK: What's in it?

SANDRA: A key.

MICK: What's that for, then?

SARA: He said to meet him there at 8:30 pm.

SANDRA: 8:30 pm? It's 8:15 pm now. I'll never make it. I've got to get Jamie to bed.

SARA: I can do that.

SANDRA (*to MICK*):
And you can help. You're not completely useless.

MICK: Yes I am.

SANDRA: You can still help!

SANDRA gets up and leaves the room.

SARA: Mum!

SARA hands her the envelope and key.

SARA: You almost forgot.

Scene 4

The Kings' house.

Later, the same evening.

MICK and SARA in kitchen. They are both slumped on chairs.

MICK: I didn't know little kids could be such hard work.

SARA: How does mum do it?

MICK: Dunno. Beats me.

SARA: Thanks anyway.

MICK: What?

SARA: You know. For helping.

MICK: Oh, that. Thanks for the beans.

SARA: You're joking?

MICK: No – they tasted well nice from the frying pan.

Pause.

SARA: Mick – do you think mum and dad are OK?

MICK: What d'you mean?

SARA: Well – that they still get on OK?

MICK: Dunno. They never see each other.

SARA: That's what I mean. Mum's down at the 3 Bs working. Dad's got his nightclubs. When he's around, she's working. When she's around, he's working. Not perfect, is it?

MICK: They seem OK to me. He just gave her a present. That key.

SARA: I suppose so. What do you reckon it's for?

MICK: Some flash, new car?

SARA: I doubt it. He tried that before. She said she didn't like the colour.

They both laugh.

SARA: Right. I've got homework to do.

MICK: Homework?

SARA: Yeah, you know. That stuff they give you at school.

MICK (*smiles*):
Never heard of it, sis.

Scene 5

Brightsea Marina.

Later, the same evening.

SANDRA outside the apartment block at Brightsea Marina. She looks along the street.

SANDRA (*reads aloud from the envelope*): '73 Harbour Court, Green Harbour Way'. This is Green Harbour Way. (*looks at the block of flats and then at the top level*) And this is Harbour Court. What's he up to?

She goes up to the closed glass entrance. There's an intercom on the wall.

SANDRA: That's it. 73.

She presses a button. She speaks into the intercom.

SANDRA: Hello? Is that you, Frankie?

There's no answer.

SANDRA: Are you going to let me in?

The door buzzes. This signals that it is open. SANDRA steps forward and pushes the door open.

SANDRA: Right. Now for the lift.

She looks around. There is a notice on the lift.

SANDRA: What? You're joking! 'Not in use'.

SANRDA looks around again.

SANDRA (*sighs*):
It'll have to be the stairs.

Scene 6

Same time.

SANDRA has entered number 73. She switches on a light. It's a posh flat with a big glass window. There is thick white carpet. Music is playing softly.

SANDRA: Hello? Is anybody here?

She turns round and looks behind her. FRANKIE steps out of the shadows at the far end of the room. SANDRA has her back to him and doesn't notice until he is right next to her. He is carrying two glasses of champagne.

FRANKIE: Surprise!

SANDRA (*screams*):
Aaarghh!

This shocks FRANKIE. He jerks forward and the champagne spills over SANDRA.

SANDRA: What are you doing? I'm soaked!

FRANKIE: Thought you might like a bit of bubbly.

SANDRA: Not down my front!

FRANKIE: Here, have mine.

SANDRA is trying to dry herself.

SANDRA: No thanks. What were you thinking of?

FRANKIE: I was thinking you might like a drink!

SANDRA: A nice cup of tea might warm me up.

FRANKIE: Cup of tea? Cup of tea? This is a class flat. You don't drink tea in here.

SANDRA: Whose is it?

FRANKIE: What? The champagne?

SANDRA: The flat!

FRANKIE: Do you like it?

SANDRA: It's very …

FRANKIE: … impressive?

SANDRA: Something like that. So, go on. Tell me. Who did you borrow it from?

FRANKIE: Borrow?

SANDRA: That bloke you had a meeting with last week?

FRANKIE: No! You don't get it, do you?

SANDRA: Get what? Look, I'm sorry, Frankie. I'm tired. My brain's tired. I haven't had any supper, I've been working and I've just walked up ten flights of stairs.

FRANKIE: The flat.

SANDRA: What about it?

FRANKIE: It's yours!

SANDRA: Mine?

FRANKIE: Well – ours. You and me.

SANDRA: You and me?

FRANKIE: No need to repeat everything I say! I bought it for *us*.

SANDRA sits down on the leather sofa.

FRANKIE: Say something.

SANDRA: I'm speechless.

FRANKIE: What do you think?

SANDRA stands up. She sighs.

SANDRA: Look, don't take this the wrong way. I mean, buying this flat's a nice thought.

FRANKIE: A nice thought? It's not a flipping birthday card!

SANDRA: Alright. A very nice thought. It's just …

FRANKIE (*getting cross*):
Go on. Spit it out!

SANDRA: Well – how can we spend time over here?

FRANKIE: What do you mean?

SANDRA: We've got kids. The kids do things. Mick's football. Jamie's friends. There's no garden here.

FRANKIE walks towards the window.

FRANKIE: There's a great view and a balcony.

SANDRA: Very suitable for Jamie.

FRANKIE turns round, angry.

FRANKIE: I go to all this trouble … spend all this money …

SANDRA: I didn't ask you to.

FRANKIE: It was a surprise.

SANDRA: You can say that again. Look, Frankie …

She touches his shoulder. He shrugs her off.

FRANKIE: Leave me alone.

SANDRA: I don't need these things. Posh flats. Cars. I want you – at home more. With me and the kids. They want to see more of you.

FRANKIE goes up to her.

FRANKIE (*quietly*): Give me the key.

SANDRA: What?

FRANKIE: Give it to me.

SANDRA hands him the key.

FRANKIE (*bitterly*): You don't want to stay here, so it'll be my place. I'll use it for meetings. No need for you to set foot in it.

SANDRA: I didn't say I didn't like it.

FRANKIE: You didn't have to.

He moves towards the window. His back is to her.

FRANKIE: Go on. Go. The kids'll be waiting.

Scene 7

The Kings' house.

Late at night.

A few lights on. MICK is in the living room on the sofa. Enter SANDRA.

SANDRA: Hi, love.

MICK: Hi, mum.

SANDRA: Sara and Jamie in bed?

MICK: Yeah. You see dad?

SANDRA: Yes.

MICK: Is he coming back here tonight?

SANDRA (*weary*):
No – I don't think so.

MICK: You alright, mum? You look …

SANDRA: Wet?

MICK: Yeah. Is it raining?

SANDRA: No. It's a long story.

SANDRA sits down on the sofa.

MICK: You sure you're OK?

SANDRA: Yes, love. I'm OK.

MICK: It's just …

SANDRA: Leave it. I'm too tired to talk about it.

MICK: OK. I get the picture. How about a drink?

SANDRA: No. It's alright. I've already had one.

MICK: What about a bite to eat?

SANDRA: Ooh love. That'd be great. I haven't eaten all evening.

MICK: What d'you want? I can't do anything fancy.

SANDRA: I don't want anything fancy. I'm fed up of fancy things. I just want something simple.

MICK: How about baked beans on toast? Special recipe. Done in the frying pan.

SANDRA: In the frying pan?

MICK: Yeah. Something wrong?

SANDRA: Nothing at all. Beans in the frying pan is perfect. Just perfect.

Glossary

beats me	I don't know
(to) blush	(to) go red in the face
bubbly	champagne (informal)
class	classy/fashionable
dunno	don't know (informal)
(to) get the picture	(to) understand
gonna	going to (informal)
gross	disgusting
impressive	stunning/making an impact
intercom	electronic device to link people in different places
(to) make a scene	(to) make a fuss
no way	no (emphatic)
no worries	no problems/OK
not my scene	not the sort of place that suits me
(to) pick someone up (in a car)	(to) collect someone (using a car)
spit it out!	don't keep silent – say whatever is on your mind!
(to) take no notice	(to) ignore
(to) turn out alright	(to) end up being OK